Table of Contents

Chapter 1: Introduction- The Double Hustle

"Opportunities don't happen. You create them." – Chris Grosser

The pulsating heart of a bustling city. Sarah wakes up before the sun rises, already running through the list of tasks in her mind. The soft chime of her alarm clock signals the beginning of another day where she transitions seamlessly from an ambitious college student to a dedicated employee. As she sips her coffee, she skims through her lecture notes for a quick revision before her morning shift. James, on the other hand, has just finished a long evening at work and heads straight to the library, preparing for a night class.

Such is the reality for a growing number of students globally. In an age of soaring tuition fees and the allure of work experience, the convergence of full-time employment and rigorous academic pursuits is becoming increasingly common. And while the task may sound Herculean, with the right mindset, tools, and strategies, it is not only feasible but also incredibly rewarding.

Navigating college while working full time is not merely about juggling two major commitments. It's about managing two distinct worlds with their own cultures, expectations, and demands. In the workplace, you may be treated as an adult, expected to take on responsibilities and make critical decisions. At college, you may be surrounded by peers who have a plethora of time for extracurricular activities, social events, and perhaps, more flexibility in their schedules.

Take Alex, for example. An IT professional by day, his evenings were filled with business administration courses. While his peers would often hang out at local eateries post-classes, discussing projects or just catching up, Alex had reports to submit and early morning meetings the next day. He felt stretched thin, straddling two worlds, yet belonged entirely to neither.

However, there's another side to the coin. With the challenges come unparalleled benefits. Many students find that their work experiences enrich their academic understanding and vice versa. Sarah, our early riser, once shared how her job in a marketing firm provided real-world examples that deepened her understanding of her marketing coursework. The classroom theories came alive when she saw them in action at work.

Similarly, the skills and discipline needed to manage both commitments can be immensely beneficial. Time management, prioritization, multitasking, and handling pressure – these are abilities that both employers and academic institutions value highly. They are also skills that stay with an individual for life, proving beneficial in various scenarios.

It's essential to understand that if you're embarking on this journey, you're not alone. Economic constraints, the desire for work experience, or even personal circumstances are pushing more individuals down this path.

A survey conducted by the National Center for Education Statistics in 2018 highlighted that over 43% of full-time students were employed. This number only increases when we look at part-time students, with over 81% juggling work and studies.

Lucy's story is one that resonates with many. A single mother, returning to college was her dream. But with bills to pay and a child to raise, not working was out of the question. Taking on a full-time job and attending evening classes, she often recounts the days she felt like giving up. But today, with a degree in hand and a well-paying job, she stands as a testament to the idea that where there's a will, there's a way.

This book is dedicated to every Sarah, James, Alex, Lucy, and countless others who dare to dream big, who challenge the conventional, and who are redefining what it means to be a student in the modern age. Over the next chapters, we will delve deep into strategies, struggles, successes, and stories of managing both a full-time job and a college workload. We aim not just to help you survive but to thrive, mastering the art of juggling responsibilities while achieving your dreams.

As we embark on this journey together, remember that every challenge faced, every late night, every early morning, and every sacrifice made is a steppingstone towards a future that promises success, resilience, and unparalleled achievement.

Chapter 2: Preparing Yourself for the Dual Challenge

"The best way to predict the future is to create it." - Abraham Lincoln

The path ahead is rugged, teetering between two worlds, each demanding your attention, your energy, and your time. Yet, just like a marathon runner spends months training before the actual race, preparation is your key to triumphing in this dual challenge.

In this chapter, we'll delve into the essential groundwork required before embarking on this journey, interweaving lessons from those who've walked this tightrope before.

Navigating college while working full-time isn't merely about time management or practical strategies (although those are crucial); it's first about preparing your mind. Drawing from the techniques of elite athletes, visualization is a powerful tool. Imagine yourself managing both roles efficiently, see yourself acing that exam and performing well in that crucial work meeting. Visualizing success helps cement your commitment and boosts motivation.

Story Insight: Tim, an accountant pursuing his MBA, created a vision board, placing it beside his desk. Pictures of graduation, snippets of his dream job, quotes from role models – it was his daily reminder of the bigger picture.

Understand that there will be moments of exhaustion, days when you feel like giving up. Recognizing this upfront rather than being blindsided later can be mentally liberating.

Story Insight: Rachel, a nurse working night shifts while studying psychology, often spoke of her '3 AM epiphanies'. Those moments when she'd question her choices but then remind herself of the reasons she started. Her mantra? "Acceptance, not resistance."

Invest time in creating a detailed weekly schedule. Allocate blocks for classes, work, study, and don't forget self-care. This visual guide can help identify any potential clashes and allows you to plan proactively.

Be upfront with your employer and professors about your commitments. Often, they'll be supportive or offer flexibility when they understand your situation.

Story Insight: Aisha, a retail manager doing her bachelor's in literature, was initially hesitant to tell her boss about her classes. When she finally did, not only did she get a slight shift adjustment, but her boss also became one of her biggest cheerleaders, often asking about her assignments and grades.

Whether it's a corner of your bedroom, a local library, or a café, having a designated study space can significantly boost productivity. Ensure it's free from distractions and has all study essentials.

Story Insight: Leo, a graphic designer, transformed his balcony into a serene study spot, complete with plants, soft lighting, and a comfortable chair. It became his sanctuary, a place where he felt calm, focused, and inspired.

Emotional and Social Readiness

Surround yourself with understanding friends, family, or colleagues. They can offer encouragement during tough times or even practical help, like sharing class notes or covering a work shift. Learn to say no. Protect your time and energy. If every weekend party or every extra work task jeopardizes your primary goals, it's okay to decline.

Story Insight: Omar, who juggled customer service roles with sociology classes, recalls the transformational power of 'no'. Initially overcommitting, he soon realized boundaries were essential. While tough at first, people began to respect his time more.

Embarking on this dual journey is much like setting out on a cross-country adventure. The better you prepare, anticipate the challenges, and equip yourself, the smoother your journey will be. It's not about foreseeing every obstacle but having the mindset and tools to tackle them as they come.

As you move forward, remember the preparation phase isn't a one-time act. Regularly revisit your strategies, adjust as needed, and most importantly, keep reminding yourself of your 'why'. Your vision, dedication, and groundwork will be the bedrock of your success in this formidable yet rewarding expedition.

Chapter 3: The Art of Time Management

"Time flies, but you're the pilot." – Michael Altshuler

Whether it's the sound of a lecture being delivered, the clicking of keys as a report gets typed, or the ever-ticking hands of a clock, time is always at the forefront of the life of a full-time worker and student. Mastering its management isn't just an advantage—it's an absolute necessity. This chapter unveils the intricate art of time management, enhanced with practical examples and narratives to guide you on this pivotal aspect of the dual journey.

Every individual is handed the same 24 hours, but what one creates out of it is a unique masterpiece. Recognizing time as an opportunity rather than a limitation sets the stage for success.

Story Insight: Jake, a bookstore owner and literature major, described time as his "blank canvas". Each hour was a stroke of paint, creating a daily picture that reflected his passions, commitments, and dreams.

Strategizing Every Second

The 4D's of Time Management:

- Do: Prioritize tasks that are both urgent and essential.

- Decide: Set a specific time for tasks that are important but not urgent.

- Delegate: Offload tasks, when possible, that are urgent but not essential.

- Delete: Eliminate tasks that are neither urgent nor essential.

Story Insight: Isabella, a hotel receptionist studying hotel management, applied the 4D's religiously. She would 'Do' her assignments, 'Decide' when to revise, 'Delegate' house chores to her roommates, and 'Delete' unnecessary social media scrolling.

Time Blocking

Instead of working with endless to-do lists, allocate specific blocks of time for tasks. This helps maintain focus and offers a realistic view of available time.

Story Insight: Raj, an IT technician pursuing software engineering, segmented his day into blocks: coding practice, work tasks, lectures, and relaxation. This ensured he never overstretched in one area at the expense of another.

Empowering Tools & Techniques

Pomodoro Technique:

Work intensely for 25 minutes, then take a 5-minute break. It keeps the mind fresh and maintains high levels of focus.

Story Insight: Ling, a chef furthering her culinary arts degree, used Pomodoro during her prep time in the kitchen and while studying. This technique made tasks less daunting and increased her efficiency.

Leveraging Technology:

Apps like 'Notion' or 'Todoist' help organize tasks, while 'Forest' promotes focused work by gamifying the process.

Story Insight: Alejandro, a car salesman diving into automotive design, leaned on apps to keep track. 'Notion' was his virtual workspace, and 'Forest' kept him away from distracting notifications during study hours.

Anticipating & Adapting

No matter how well you plan, life is unpredictable. The ability to adapt is as crucial as meticulous planning. Always include buffer periods in your schedule. These can absorb unforeseen delays or provide a much-needed breather. Regularly assess your time management strategies. Are they still effective? Can anything be improved?

Story Insight: Tariq, a pharmacist delving into molecular biology, held fortnightly reviews. Looking back at his weeks, he'd pinpoint what worked and what didn't, refining his approach continually.

Navigating the winding paths of full-time work and college requires the finesse of a skilled artist, painting each second with purpose and intention. Time management isn't merely about squeezing tasks into hours but molding each moment to serve your grand vision. As you practice and perfect this art, you'll discover not just academic and professional success but also the profound satisfaction of a life well-lived.

Chapter 4: Balancing Job Responsibilities with Academic Demands

"Life is an act of balancing forces. It's how we handle challenges that defines who we are." - Ellen DeGeneres

Treading the fine line between professional commitments and academic pursuits can often feel like a high-wire act. The delicate balance of giving your best in both spheres, without letting one topple the other, is challenging yet essential. This chapter offers a compass, guiding you through this balancing act, enriched with tangible strategies and heartfelt stories from those who have been on this journey.

Before diving into balancing techniques, it's crucial to comprehend the nature of the two worlds you're straddling. Full-time jobs, even with their demanding moments, often have structured hours, predictable tasks, and a familiar environment. College, on the other hand, has fluctuating demands—quiet weeks leading up to stormy periods of assignments, exams, and projects.

Story Insight: Aditi, a marketing executive and part-time MBA student, described her experience as "sailing calm seas with sudden turbulent storms." Understanding this rhythm, she proactively planned for the academic 'storms' during her work's calmer days.

Synchronizing Two Worlds

Inform both your employer and your professors about your dual commitments. They may offer leniencies, extensions, or even advice to help you. Identify areas where your job and studies align. Can a project at work double as a class assignment? Can job experiences be leveraged for class discussions?

Story Insight: Fiona, a junior architect pursuing an advanced design course, utilized her office projects as case studies. Her real-world applications earned accolades from professors and peers alike.

Break your day into detailed blocks—morning routines, commute, lunch breaks, etc. Even a 20-minute window can be used for quick revision or email checks. Combine your work and academic schedules, marking deadlines, meetings, exams, etc. This way, you can preemptively see if any clashes are on the horizon. Designate study hours post-work and stick to them. Avoid bringing work home or letting academic assignments spill into office hours.

Story Insight: Jackson, a tech support agent delving into software development, had a strict rule: post 8 PM was study-time. This non-negotiable boundary ensured he dedicated time to academics daily.

Ironically, a pivotal aspect of balancing work and studies is understanding the importance of pauses. Integrate regular, short breaks into your schedule. It prevents burnout, rejuvenates the mind, and boosts productivity. Dedicate at least a portion of your weekends to relaxation—whether it's pursuing a hobby, spending time with loved ones, or simply catching up on sleep.

Story Insight: Tomas, an event manager studying arts and culture, cherished his Sunday mornings. Unplugged from all responsibilities, he'd paint, transforming stress into strokes of color on canvas.

Balancing professional and academic demands isn't about perpetually juggling or sacrificing one for the other. Instead, it's a dance of synchronization, anticipation, and rejuvenation. As you refine this balance, you not only ensure success in both spheres but also cultivate the invaluable skills of adaptability, resilience, and resourcefulness.

Chapter 5: The Importance of Setting Priorities

"Action expresses priorities." – Mahatma Gandhi

In a world swirling with tasks, responsibilities, and countless distractions, how does one navigate towards genuine progress and fulfillment? The answer is surprisingly simple, yet profound: by setting priorities. This chapter delves into the art and science of determining what truly matters, underlining the role of prioritization in shaping one's journey between full-time work and college. Enriched with relatable narratives and actionable insights, we invite you to explore the transformative power of priorities.

Before diving deep into the strategies, it's paramount to understand the essence of setting priorities. Imagine trying to navigate a vast ocean without a compass—prioritization offers that guiding direction in the vast sea of responsibilities and aspirations.

Story Insight: Eleanor, a librarian, and a student of literature, likens her priorities to her "North Star". She said, "Whenever I felt overwhelmed, I'd look to my priorities, and they'd illuminate my path, guiding me through the densest fogs of confusion."

Start with the end in mind. What do you aim to achieve professionally and academically? This vision will act as a filter, helping you discern essential tasks from the noise. The Eisenhower Matrix, a tool that categorizes tasks based on urgency and importance, is invaluable. Learn to focus on what's important, even if it isn't urgent, to prevent last-minute scrambles.

Story Insight: Mia, an accountant pursuing her Master's, had a mantra: "Tackle the important before they become urgent." She always preemptively worked on major assignments, ensuring she wasn't overwhelmed when deadlines approached.

While it's essential to prioritize, it's equally important to be adaptable. Identify areas of rigidity (immutable deadlines) and areas of flexibility (tasks that can be rescheduled). Where do your job and academics intertwine? Identifying and leveraging these overlaps can save time and effort.

Story Insight: Clarisse, working in sales while studying psychology, often used her understanding of human behavior from her classes to enhance her sales pitches, making her studies immediately applicable and prioritized.

Tools & Techniques for Effective Prioritization

The ABCD Method:

- *A: Essential tasks that must be done immediately.*

- *B: Important tasks that can wait for a short time.*

- *C: Tasks that can be postponed or even delegated.*

- *D: Tasks to be deleted or avoided to save time.*

Story Insight: Rajan, a graphics designer studying visual arts, color-coded his to-do lists based on the ABCD method. This vibrant visual cue helped him intuitively know where to direct his energies.

Understand that 80% of results often come from 20% of the efforts. Identify that crucial 20% in both work and academics to maximize output. Prioritization isn't just about organizing tasks; it's about aligning actions with visions and values. When priorities are clear, decision-making becomes effortless, distractions fade, and progress becomes palpable.

Chapter 6: Building a Support System: Friends, Family, and Colleagues

"Individuals play the game, but teams win championships." - Bill Parcells

Embarking on the demanding journey of balancing full-time work with academic pursuits is not a solo venture. The weight of responsibilities can be made lighter by sharing, understanding, and collaboration. In the labyrinth of challenges and deadlines, a strong support system acts as your safety net, guiding light, and cheering squad. This chapter accentuates the importance of fostering and nurturing relationships with friends, family, and colleagues, demonstrating how they become crucial pillars in your academic and professional journey. Understanding the role your support system plays provide clarity on why building and maintaining it is vital.

Story Insight: Rosa, a paralegal studying law, felt isolated and overwhelmed, juggling work and studies alone. A casual chat with a colleague led to the discovery that they were both in similar situations. By simply sharing experiences and collaborating on study schedules, they both felt more connected and less burdened.

Friends, especially those in similar situations, can offer empathetic understanding, camaraderie, and shared resources like notes or study groups. Friends can hold you accountable for your academic goals, pushing you when you feel demotivated.

Story Insight: Layla, a journalist pursuing a master's in communication, had a pact with her best friend. They'd share weekly goals and check on each other's progress, creating a cycle of motivation and responsibility.

Family provides a safe space, offering comfort during stressful times and celebrating your achievements. Family can sometimes chip in with daily tasks, giving you the breathing space to focus on work or studies.

Story Insight: Ananya, a retail manager studying business analytics, was grateful to her sister, who often helped with household chores, allowing Ananya extra hours of undisturbed study.

Understanding colleagues can cover for you during crunch academic periods if you've built a rapport and reciprocity. Colleagues, especially those with academic backgrounds, can provide valuable insights, resources, or mentorship.

Story Insight: Fatima, an engineer branching into advanced robotics, frequently consulted with a senior colleague who had completed a similar course. His guidance often provided clarity and direction in her academic pursuits.

Keep your support system informed about your commitments, challenges, and achievements. Their understanding of your situation deepens with transparent communication. A support system isn't a one-way street. Offer help, gratitude, and be there for them, fostering mutual respect and understanding. Despite a packed schedule, carve out moments for your friends, family, and colleagues. Shared memories strengthen bonds.

Building a support system isn't merely about surrounding yourself with people, but about cultivating relationships anchored in trust, understanding, and mutual growth. As you traverse the intricate paths of work and academia, these relationships will be the wind beneath your wings, the cushion during falls, and the joy in every milestone.

Chapter 7: Sleep, Health, and Well-being: Non-Negotiables

"It is health that is real wealth and not pieces of gold and silver." - Mahatma Gandhi

Amid deadlines and responsibilities, there's an element often compromised yet indispensable: health. As you navigate the dual terrains of work and academics, physical and mental well-being can easily fall by the wayside. However, the quality of your health—mental, emotional, and physical—directly influences your capacity to perform and persevere. This chapter underscores the critical nature of sleep, general health, and holistic well-being, drawing attention to their role as non-negotiables in your journey.

Sleep: The Underrated Fuel

Sleep is vital for cognitive functions like memory, attention, and problem-solving, all of which are crucial for both work and academic success. Adequate sleep ensures emotional stability, reducing susceptibility to stress and enhancing resilience.

Story Insight: Nadia, a nurse pursuing further qualifications, noticed her irritability and emotional outbursts were directly proportional to her lack of sleep. A commitment to regular sleep transformed her emotional landscape, benefiting her professional and academic life.

Regular exercise and a balanced diet enhance stamina, crucial for long hours of work and study. Proper nutrition and exercise bolster the immune system, reducing sick days and ensuring consistent performance. Practices like meditation, deep breathing, and journaling can help navigate the mental challenges of balancing work and study.

Story Insight: Aarav, a software developer diving into advanced algorithms, took up daily meditation. The clarity and calmness he derived transformed his approach to challenges, making him more solution oriented.

It's okay to seek therapy or counseling when overwhelmed. Mental health professionals can provide coping mechanisms and strategies.

Story Insight: Lina, a marketing executive pursuing an MBA, felt engulfed by anxiety. Counseling sessions provided her with tools to manage her anxiety, ensuring it didn't hinder her ambitions.

Make sleep, exercise, and mental well-being practices a part of your daily routine, ensuring consistency. Recognize signs of fatigue, stress, or burnout. Adjust your schedule or seek help when needed. Stay informed about health and well-being practices. As your journey evolves, so should your health strategies.

This chapter seeks to drive home a foundational truth: your health is the bedrock upon which the edifice of your aspirations stands. Neglecting it can lead to cracks in the foundation, jeopardizing everything you're working towards. Through narratives and insights, we hope to inspire readers to treat their health—be it sleep, physical well-being, or mental health—as non-negotiable. For in the harmony of mind, body, and soul lies the symphony of success and fulfillment.

Chapter 8: The Financial Advantages of Working Full-Time

"Do not save what is left after spending, but spend what is left after saving." - Warren Buffett

As you split your time between the professional world and the academic arena, there's an underlying silver lining—financial advantages. Holding a full-time job while pursuing education offers a unique blend of monetary benefits. This chapter aims to spotlight these financial boons, elucidating how they can be harnessed to achieve both short-term and long-term goals.

A consistent salary can significantly ease the burden of tuition fees, books, and other academic expenses, reducing or even eliminating the need for student loans. Regular earnings can support a comfortable lifestyle, covering rent, utilities, transportation, and more, without resorting to the stereotypical cash-strapped student life.

Story Insight: Lee, a graphic designer, while pursuing his degree, enjoyed the freedom of choosing a comfortable apartment closer to both his workplace and university, all thanks to his job.

Having a steady income allows you to build an emergency fund, providing a safety net for unforeseen financial hurdles. With a consistent income, you can start investing earlier, harnessing the power of compound interest, and creating a foundation for future wealth.

Story Insight: Clara, a sales executive studying marketing, began investing a small portion of her salary in stocks and mutual funds. By the time she graduated, her portfolio had grown, giving her a head start in financial planning.

Many full-time positions come with health insurance, saving you significant amounts on medical expenses. Early contributions to retirement accounts, especially if matched by employers, can lead to substantial growth over time. Managing a full-time salary while studying instills budgeting skills and financial discipline, which are invaluable life skills. Earning and managing your money offers a genuine understanding of the value of hard work, money, and the importance of informed financial decisions.

Story Insight: Ling, a tech support specialist studying IT solutions, once splurged her monthly salary on gadgets. The subsequent tight budget month taught her the significance of judicious spending.

While the challenges of juggling work and studies are evident, the financial advantages are undeniable. This chapter illuminates the myriad ways in which a full-time job can bolster your financial stability, freedom, and literacy. With stories and insights, the aim is to inspire you to recognize, appreciate, and maximize these monetary benefits, setting the stage for a future of financial empowerment and success.

Chapter 9: Study Strategies for the Busy Student

"Success is no accident. It is hard work, perseverance, learning, studying, sacrifice and most of all, love of what you are doing or learning to do." - Pelé

Juggling full-time work with academic aspirations can feel like a Herculean task. One of the most crucial aspects of this balance is mastering the art of efficient studying. With limited time and a myriad of distractions, the importance of effective study techniques cannot be stressed enough. This chapter delves deep into study strategies tailored for those with tight schedules, offering insights, anecdotes, and actionable tips to transform your academic journey.

Focused Sessions: Quality over Quantity

The Pomodoro Technique:

Using a timer, study intensively for 25 minutes and then take a 5-minute break. This helps maintain concentration and reduces burnout.

Avoid Multitasking:

Focus on one subject or topic at a time. Multitasking can diminish concentration and retention.

Story Insight: Tom, an IT professional branching into cybersecurity, initially tried juggling multiple subjects. Recognizing the pitfalls of multitasking, he adjusted to monotasking, reaping immediate benefits in comprehension.

Active Learning: Engage to Retain

Teach to Learn:

After studying a topic, try explaining it to someone else. Teaching reinforces understanding.

Story Insight: Priya, a nurse upskilling in pediatrics, formed a study group where members taught each other. This active learning approach cemented her knowledge.

Mind Maps & Visualization:

Visual tools can help structure information and improve memory.

Story Insight: Jamal, an architect exploring urban planning, began using mind maps to connect concepts. This visual technique enriched his grasp and recall of complex topics.

Technology & Tools: Modern Allies

Study Apps & Platforms:

Apps like Quizlet, Anki, or Khan Academy can aid in revision and concept clarity.

Story Insight: Mei, a marketing expert venturing into data analytics, harnessed Quizlet for flashcards and quizzes, streamlining her revision process.

Digital Calendars & Scheduling:

Tools like Google Calendar can help in setting study schedules, ensuring consistency.

Story Insight: Carlos, a chef mastering culinary arts, meticulously scheduled his study sessions. Digital reminders kept him on track, maximizing his learning outcome.

Environment & Setting: The Unsung Heroes

Dedicated Study Space:

Create a dedicated, distraction-free space for studying to boost concentration.

Story Insight: Aisha, an HR professional studying organizational behavior, transformed a corner of her apartment into a study nook. This dedicated space became her sanctuary of focus.

Ambient Noise & Music:

Some people find background noise or specific music genres, like classical music, conducive to studying.

Story Insight: Leo, a mechanic engrossed in automotive technology, found solace in ambient cafe sounds, which surprisingly amplified his concentration levels.

Regular Review & Spaced Repetition

Consistent Revision:

Reviewing notes regularly, rather than cramming, aids in long-term retention.

Story Insight: Fatima, a paralegal diving into corporate law, adopted a routine of daily mini-revisions. This habit transformed her exam preparations, making them less stressful and more effective.

Spaced Repetition:

Revisiting information at increasing intervals reinforces memory.

Story Insight: Sergei, a software developer branching into AI, leveraged spaced repetition apps. This technique drastically improved his recall during crucial presentations.

The role of efficient studying in a time-crunched life is paramount. This chapter, filled with strategies, stories, and tips, aims to equip you with tools that tailor the vast world of academics to your unique schedule. With the right techniques, even the busiest student can achieve academic excellence without compromising on work commitments.

Chapter 10: Maximizing Downtime: Study on Breaks, Lunch, and Commutes

"Lost time is never found again." - Benjamin Franklin

In the high-speed life of someone balancing work and academics, every minute counts. However, many of us overlook the treasure troves of time hidden within our daily routines. This chapter explores the art of utilizing these pockets of downtime – breaks, lunch hours, and commutes – and converting them into productive study sessions.

Breaks: Mini Study Sessions

Quick Flashcards Review:

Keep a deck of flashcards handy for a rapid review of key concepts.

Mindfulness and Reflection:

Use short breaks to mentally recap lessons, solidifying your understanding.

Story Insight: Arjun, an engineer studying for his Master's, would close his eyes during breaks and mentally walk through what he'd learned the previous night.

Lunch Hour: A Golden Hour

Audiobooks and Podcasts:

If you can't read, listen! Many textbooks are available in audio format, as are educational podcasts on various subjects.

Story Insight: Lila, a dietician transitioning to holistic health, listened to nutrition podcasts during her lunch walks.

Discussion Groups:

If colleagues are also studying, form a lunch-hour study group. Discussing can help reinforce learning.

Story Insight: Rashid and Sophia, both in the same software firm and online course, would discuss weekly topics over lunch, clarifying doubts and deepening understanding.

Commutes: Traveling with Knowledge

Mobile E-Learning Platforms:

Platforms like Coursera, Udemy, and Khan Academy offer mobile-friendly courses you can access on-the-go.

Story Insight: Sergio, a sales rep with an hour-long train commute, completed entire modules on his tablet during his daily travels.

Language Learning:

If you're learning a new language, commutes are perfect for practicing pronunciation and vocabulary using apps like Duolingo or Babbel.

Story Insight: Hana, a hotel manager learning French for her job, would practice speaking during her drive to work, improving her accent and fluency.

Making the Most of Waiting Times

E-Books and Online Journals:

Carry e-books or access online journals on your mobile or tablet. Waiting in line or for an appointment can become an opportunity.

Story Insight: Alex, a physiotherapist diving into sports medicine, would read articles while waiting for his clients, keeping up to date with the latest research.

Brain Training Apps:

Use apps like Lumosity or Elevate to enhance cognitive skills, improving overall learning efficiency.

Story Insight: Farah, an art director exploring design theory, enjoyed brain-training games during her metro rides, refining her problem-solving and focus.

Consistency is Key

Regularly Schedule Downtime:

Make it a habit to consistently use your downtime for studying. Even if it's just a few minutes, it accumulates over time.

Story Insight: Chen, an accountant branching into financial analytics, had a strict rule: every bus ride home was for studying. This routine added hours of learning to his week.

Stay Adaptable:

If one method doesn't work, try another. The goal is to find what suits your rhythm and lifestyle.

Story Insight: Omar, an event planner delving into public relations, initially tried podcasts but found e-books more his pace during lunch breaks.

Embedded in our bustling days are pockets of downtime, waiting to be transformed into productive intervals. This chapter illuminates methods, tools, and real-life anecdotes that showcase how these moments can be converted into opportunities for academic growth. By recognizing and harnessing these intervals, even the most time-pressed individual can effectively pave their path to academic success.

Chapter 11: Course Selection and Scheduling for Success

"It's not enough to be busy; so are the ants. The question is: what are we busy about?" - Henry David Thoreau

A cornerstone of college success, especially for those juggling full-time work, is smart course selection and meticulous scheduling. This chapter unveils the nuances of selecting the right courses and scheduling them optimally, weaving in personal anecdotes to bring the narrative to life.

Strategic Course Selection: Laying the Foundation

Evaluate Your Strengths and Weaknesses:

Understand which subjects or courses you naturally excel in and which may require extra time or resources.

Story Insight: Naomi, an IT specialist returning to college for her Master's, loved coding but struggled with theory. She strategically enrolled in theoretical modules during lighter work periods.

Consider Course Format and Delivery:

Does the course offer online modules? Is it seminar-based or lecture-driven? The format can greatly affect manageability.

Story Insight: Elijah, a retail manager pursuing a degree in Business Administration, opted for courses that provided online lectures. This allowed him to engage during his off-hours.

Balancing Workload: The Jigsaw Puzzle

Diversify Course Difficulty:

Don't overload a semester with all challenging subjects. Mix and match for a balanced academic workload.

Story Insight: Priyanka, an administrative assistant studying literature, paired complex subjects like "Renaissance Literature" with lighter ones like "Modern Poetry" to ensure balanced semesters.

Beware of Prerequisites:

Ensure you've met all prerequisites before enrolling. This prevents potential scheduling conflicts or overburdening in subsequent semesters.

Story Insight: Javier, an engineer venturing into advanced physics, mistakenly overlooked a key prerequisite. This blunder postponed his advanced modules, causing undue stress.

Scheduling for Success: Time is Your Ally

Avoid Back-to-Back Classes:

Allow breaks between classes, ensuring time for rest, review, and unexpected work demands.

Story Insight: Leila, a paralegal branching into international law, initially had back-to-back classes. This left her drained, with little time for revision. Spreading them out enhanced her focus and retention.

Leverage Technology:

Digital planners like Google Calendar or Trello can be lifesavers. Set reminders, plot out study times, and sync with your work schedule.

Story Insight: Andre, a graphic designer studying visual communication, diligently mapped his academic and work schedules on Trello. This gave him a holistic view, helping avoid clashes and over-commitments.

Seek Counsel and Stay Updated

Engage Academic Advisors:

Regularly consult academic counselors. They can provide invaluable insights into course demands, sequencing, and potential pitfalls.

Story Insight: Rosa, a nurse aiming for a specialization, initially underestimated the workload of her chosen courses. Regular sessions with her advisor allowed her to re-strategize and prioritize modules effectively.

Join Student Forums or Groups:

Engaging with peers can provide real-time reviews and tips on courses, professors, and scheduling.

Story Insight: Ken, a marketer exploring digital trends, joined a student forum. Insights from senior students on course difficulty and professor teaching styles proved instrumental in his decision-making.

Course selection and scheduling are akin to setting the stage for your college journey. This chapter, enriched with strategies and real-life accounts, aims to guide you through the maze of choices, leading to a path that complements your work life. By making informed decisions and optimizing schedules, you can create a college experience that's not only manageable but also immensely rewarding.

Chapter 12: Effective Communication with Professors and Employers

"The single biggest problem in communication is the illusion that it has taken place." - George Bernard Shaw

Managing a college education while holding a full-time job necessitates navigating two distinct realms simultaneously. Within these spheres, effective communication with both professors and employers becomes paramount. This chapter delves into the subtleties of this dialogue, interspersed with real-life stories for deeper resonance.

The Academic Realm: Speaking with Professors

Initiate Early:

At the semester's onset, inform professors of your full-time job. This proactive approach sets a foundation for mutual understanding.

Story Insight: Amara, a social worker pursuing sociology, always sent a concise email at the start, explaining her work situation. This preemptive move often fostered a supportive rapport with her educators.

Seek Clarity:

If you're unsure about coursework or scheduling, ask promptly. Professors appreciate engaged and inquisitive students.

Story Insight: Keegan, an architect delving into sustainable design, once misunderstood an assignment's requirements. Clarifying with the professor not only rectified his course but also demonstrated his commitment.

Stay Respectful and Professional:

Always maintain decorum. Address professors appropriately, respond promptly, and honor set appointments.

Story Insight: Jade, a journalist studying international relations, made it a point to always address her professors with their preferred titles and showed gratitude for their time, which left a lasting positive impression.

The Professional Arena: Conversing with Employers

Open the Dialogue:

It's essential to inform your employer about your educational pursuits, ensuring they understand the demands you'll face.

Story Insight: Rafael, a tech analyst undertaking a data science program, discussed his academic journey with his boss, who appreciated the transparency and even provided flexible hours on class days.

Find the Win-Win:

Highlight how your education benefits the company – be it through skill acquisition or broadened networks.

Story Insight: Marianne, a hotel manager pursuing hospitality marketing, shared insights from her coursework in team meetings. Her employer saw direct value, leading to increased support for her studies.

Address Concerns Proactively:

If you foresee a clash between work commitments and academic obligations, communicate early and suggest potential solutions.

Story Insight: Sameer, a software developer enrolling in an AI course, realized a major project deadline clashed with his finals. By addressing this early, his team redistributed tasks, ensuring both commitments were met.

The Interlink: Managing Dual Commitments

Calendar Sync:

Keep an integrated calendar for work and academic schedules. This visual aid can prevent overcommitments and clashes.

Story Insight: Clara, a financial planner studying behavioral economics, used Google Calendar to overlay her work and academic timelines. This integration helped her foresee and navigate busy periods.

Regular Check-ins:

Periodically review your standing with both professors and employers. Address any brewing concerns promptly.

Story Insight: Jerome, a chef branching into nutrition science, had monthly check-ins with his head chef and course mentor, ensuring he was on track and making necessary adjustments when required.

Effective communication is the bridge that ensures smooth passage through the demanding terrains of both work and education. This chapter, enriched with strategies and illustrative narratives, seeks to equip you with the tools and awareness to foster understanding and support in both domains. By cultivating this dialogue, you pave the way for a synergistic balance, where both your professional and academic aspirations can coalesce and thrive.

Chapter 13: The Online Course Advantage

"The capacity to learn is a gift; the ability to learn is a skill; the willingness to learn is a choice." - Brian Herbert

As the digital age unfurls, online courses are emerging as a godsend for those balancing employment with education. The flexibility, accessibility, and array of online options can be instrumental in harmonizing the demands of work and studies. Let's journey through the benefits of online courses, interspersed with evocative stories for deeper understanding.

The Flexibility Quotient

Self-Paced Learning:

Most online courses offer modules that students can traverse at their convenience, allowing for a tailored study rhythm.

Story Insight: Layla, a flight attendant with erratic schedules, cherished online courses. Their self-paced nature let her delve into anthropology lectures between flights, optimizing her fragmented free hours.

No Geographical Constraints:

Learn from anywhere! Whether from a café, your office, or your living room, online courses eradicate geographical barriers.

Story Insight: Carlos, a field engineer often stationed in remote locations, could pursue his dream of studying environmental science thanks to online classes, which he accessed even from the heart of forests.

Diverse Course Offerings & Global Perspectives

Expansive Subject Choices:

With institutions worldwide offering online courses, you're not restricted by local curriculum limitations.

Story Insight: Min, an accountant in Seoul, was passionate about Brazilian literature. Online platforms allowed her to enroll in specialized courses from Brazilian universities, broadening her horizons.

Engage with International Cohorts:

Interact with peers from various corners of the globe, enriching discussions with diverse perspectives.

Story Insight: Ahmed, studying global politics online, valued debates with classmates from six continents. Their varied backgrounds brought richness and depth to discussions on geopolitical dynamics.

Cost-Efficient & Resource-Rich

Often Economical:

Without infrastructure and overhead costs, many online courses tend to be more affordable than their traditional counterparts.

Story Insight: Sarah, a single mother and retail supervisor, was deterred by the high tuition fees of traditional colleges. Discovering more affordable online alternatives, she embarked on her psychology studies without straining her finances.

Abundant Resources:

Online platforms often brim with supplementary materials – from forums to e-books, enhancing the learning experience.

Story Insight: Arvind, delving into ancient civilizations, reveled in the plethora of resources his online platform provided. E-books, seminars, and forums enriched his understanding beyond just the curriculum.

Cultivating Discipline & Tech Skills

Self-Motivation & Responsibility:

The autonomy of online courses necessitates self-discipline, inadvertently refining your organizational and time-management skills.

Story Insight: Tasha, a startup founder, found her online MBA demanding in terms of self-regulation. This discipline spilled over, enhancing her managerial skills in her enterprise.

Tech-Savviness:

Navigating online platforms, using digital tools, and troubleshooting minor tech issues can amplify your digital proficiency.

Story Insight: Leo, a history teacher transitioning to digital marketing, realized that his online courses did more than just impart marketing knowledge. They also elevated his digital skills, making him more market-ready.

The digital realm has revolutionized education, making it more accessible and adaptable. This chapter, peppered with strategies and real-life tales, champions the online course avenue for full-time workers. By harnessing the digital advantage, you can weave in academic pursuits seamlessly with your professional life, crafting a tapestry of continual growth and fulfillment.

Chapter 14: Group Projects and Teamwork: Making it Work with a Tight Schedule

"Alone we can do so little; together we can do so much." - Helen Keller

Group projects: A quintessential aspect of academic life that either fosters collaboration or cultivates frustration. For a full-time worker, this aspect of collegiate life becomes even more challenging. Balancing work, personal commitments, and collaborative academic tasks requires finesse and strategy. This chapter navigates the nuanced terrains of group endeavors, weaving in real-life tales for deeper understanding.

The Prelude: Setting the Right Tone

Initiate Communication:

At the project's onset, communicate your work commitments to your group. An early heads-up paves the way for understanding and adaptability.

Story Insight: Nathan, a bank manager pursuing business analytics, always initiated a group meet to discuss his limited availability during work hours. His transparency led to planned schedules accommodating everyone's commitments.

Selecting Roles Wisely:

Choose project roles aligning with your strengths and time constraints. If your work schedule is unpredictable, avoid critical time-sensitive tasks.

Story Insight: Aisha, a nurse with varying shifts, opted for tasks she could manage independently, like research or report writing, ensuring her erratic schedule didn't impede group progress.

The Planning Phase: Organized Efficiency

Leverage Technology:

Use digital tools like Trello or Slack for task tracking, scheduling, and communication, allowing for smooth virtual collaboration.

Story Insight: Miguel, an IT consultant delving into cybersecurity, introduced his group to Asana. This tool helped the team stay in sync, track progress, and facilitate communication, irrespective of physical meetups.

Set Clear Deadlines:

With multiple schedules in play, establish interim deadlines. This ensures timely progress and provides buffer periods for unforeseen delays.

Story Insight: Elise, a store manager studying retail strategies, insisted on setting individual task deadlines a week before the actual submission. This buffer allowed for last-minute changes without the stress of impending deadlines.

The Execution: Adaptive Collaboration

Opt for Virtual Meetups:

If physical meetings are challenging, Zoom or Skype can be effective alternatives, ensuring regular touchpoints.

Story Insight: Jae, a pilot studying aviation management, often found himself in different time zones. Virtual meetups were his saving grace, allowing him to contribute actively despite geographical constraints.

Share Resources Digitally:

Platforms like Google Drive or Dropbox facilitate seamless sharing of resources, making collaboration efficient and paperless.

Story Insight: Sofia, a journalist diving into multimedia storytelling, created shared folders for her group. This ensured everyone had access to the latest materials, fostering a cohesive work process.

The Finale: Wrapping up with Grace

Seek Feedback:

After submission, gather feedback on the collaboration process. This aids in refining strategies for future group projects.

Story Insight: Dev, a theater artist exploring scriptwriting, always held a post-submission group chat. Discussing the highs and lows of their collaborative journey helped him gain insights for future teamwork.

Show Gratitude:

A simple thank you goes a long way. Recognize and appreciate the efforts of your teammates.

Story Insight: Lila, a chef branching into nutrition, made it a ritual to pen thank-you notes post project, acknowledging the adaptability and patience of her teammates. This small gesture often solidified her rapport for future collaborations.

Group projects, while challenging, can be made manageable with clear communication, efficient planning, and adaptive strategies. This chapter, interspersed with tales and tips, seeks to equip full-time workers with the tools to seamlessly integrate collaborative academic tasks into their packed lives. By fostering mutual understanding and leveraging digital tools, you can transform group endeavors from hurdles into valuable learning experiences.

Chapter 15: Handling Setbacks: When Life Throws a Curveball

"Success is not final, failure is not fatal: It is the courage to continue that counts." – Winston Churchill

Life, with its unpredictable nature, is often interlaced with setbacks. For someone juggling work with studies, these setbacks can sometimes feel insurmountable. Yet, as the axiom goes, it's not about how many times you fall, but how many times you get up. This chapter delves into managing setbacks, illustrated with relatable stories, offering solace and strategies to navigate turbulent times.

Understanding Setbacks: A Broader Perspective

Inevitability of Life's Hiccups:

Recognize that setbacks are natural life occurrences, not a reflection of one's capability or worth.

Story Insight: Reena, a corporate executive delving into finance, faced an unexpected project failure at work.

Instead of berating herself, she viewed it as a natural hiccup, a stance that aided her recovery and subsequent successes.

Growth in Adversity:

Often, the most profound personal and professional growth stems from challenging times.

Story Insight: Jamal, a store owner studying business development, saw his business nosedive. Yet, this setback led him to innovate, ultimately setting the foundation for an even more prosperous venture.

Practical Steps: Navigating the Storm

Seek Support:

Reach out to mentors, friends, or professionals. Sometimes, a listening ear or an alternate perspective can make all the difference.

Story Insight: Mei, a nurse pursuing advanced medicinal studies, struggled with an overwhelming course load. Seeking guidance from her professor, she received not just academic support but also emotional backing, making her journey smoother.

Re-evaluate & Prioritize:

A setback can be an opportunity to reassess your goals, strategies, and commitments, recalibrating for a clearer path forward.

Story Insight: Ivan, an engineer exploring sustainable technologies, faced ridicule for an unconventional project idea. Taking a step back, he refined his concept, which later garnered accolades in an international forum.

Emotional Wellness: The Heart of Recovery

Allow Yourself to Grieve:

Recognize your emotions, be it disappointment, anger, or sadness. By acknowledging these feelings, you create space for healing.

Story Insight: Maria, a teacher branching into counseling, received a setback in her thesis approval. She allowed herself to grieve, an emotional release that paved the way for renewed vigor.

Maintain Self-Care Rituals:

Ensure that setbacks don't derail your routines, be it exercise, meditation, or hobbies. These rituals can be therapeutic anchors.

Story Insight: Suleiman, a journalist venturing into documentary filmmaking, faced funding rejections. His daily morning runs became his therapeutic escape, helping him maintain mental equilibrium.

Bouncing Back: Resilience in Action

Adopt a Growth Mindset:

Embrace challenges as learning experiences. Instead of viewing setbacks as failures, see them as opportunities for growth.

Story Insight: Clara, a software developer diving into AI, faced multiple algorithm failures. Adopting a growth mindset, she viewed each failure as a lesson, eventually leading her to groundbreaking success.

Celebrate Small Wins:

In the aftermath of a setback, every small victory counts. Recognize and celebrate these moments, fueling your motivation.

Story Insight: Diego, an artist exploring avant-garde art, faced criticism for a bold project. Undeterred, he celebrated smaller gallery inclusions, using them as stepping stones to larger triumphs.

Setbacks, though daunting, can be transformed into stepping stones with the right mindset and strategies. This chapter, a melange of tales and tools, aspires to guide those grappling with challenges, helping them metamorphose setbacks into setups for grander successes. Through understanding, emotional wellness, and proactive strategies, you can navigate life's curveballs with grace and resilience.

Chapter 16: Using Workplace Skills in the Classroom (and Vice Versa)

"The future belongs to those who learn more skills and combine them in creative ways." - Robert Greene

One of the unique advantages of being both a student and a full-time worker is the ability to shuttle skills between the workplace and the classroom. But how can one recognize and adeptly transfer these skills? This chapter breaks down this bi-directional transfer, interlacing insights with real-life stories, thereby illuminating pathways for holistic growth.

The Synergy of Skills: Recognizing the Overlap

Transferable Skills:

Core competencies such as communication, problem-solving, and time management have universal applicability, regardless of context.

Story Insight: Elena, a marketing executive studying psychology, harnessed her presentation skills from work to lead captivating class presentations, often receiving standing ovations.

Adapting to Diverse Environments:

The versatility cultivated by adapting to both academic and professional environments can be a formidable asset.

Story Insight: Farid, an architect exploring urban planning, utilized his workplace adaptability to easily transition between group projects at college and collaborative designs at work.

From Workplace to Classroom: Bringing Professional Prowess to Academia

Project Management:

Overseeing projects at work can enhance your ability to handle academic assignments, ensuring timely and quality submissions.

Story Insight: Layla, a project manager delving into environmental sciences, adeptly applied her work strategies to orchestrate her semester research, culminating in a university accolade.

Networking Skills:

Leveraging professional contacts can offer unique insights or resources for academic endeavors.

Story Insight: Raj, a sales manager pursuing global business, tapped into his international contacts for firsthand insights on his thesis, adding a richness that textbooks couldn't provide.

From Classroom to Workplace: Academic Acumen in Professional Settings

Research Proficiency:

Rigorous academic research can refine your ability to gather and analyze data, a skill invaluable in many professional spheres.

Story Insight: Ying, a statistician branching into market research, used her academic research acumen to unveil market patterns, elevating her company's strategy.

Ethical Considerations:

Academic settings often emphasize ethical considerations, a perspective that can enhance workplace decisions.

Story Insight: Carlos, a lawyer studying human rights, incorporated his classroom learnings on ethics to drive more humane legal strategies, garnering appreciation from clients.

The Mutual Enrichment: Continuous Learning & Growth

Lifelong Learning:

The interplay between academic and professional realms fosters continuous learning, keeping you updated and adaptable.

Story Insight: Naomi, a tech developer exploring neuromorphic engineering, kept herself at the industry's forefront, weaving academic novelties into her professional innovations.

Broadened Horizons:

The dual exposure to workplace and academia can broaden your horizons, encouraging interdisciplinary thinking.

Story Insight: Hakim, a journalist venturing into digital media strategies, merged storytelling with digital tools, crafting engaging narratives that skyrocketed his articles' viewership.

Mastering the art of shuttling skills between the workplace and the classroom is akin to maintaining a balanced ecosystem—each realm nourishes the other. This chapter, interspersed with tales and techniques, aims to shed light on this intricate dance of skill transfer. By recognizing the synergies and consciously integrating them, you can evolve into a multifaceted professional and scholar, reaping the benefits of dual worlds.

Chapter 17: Building Your Professional Network While in College

"Succeeding in life is all about building the right relationships." – John C. Maxwell

As the adage goes, "It's not just what you know, but who you know." Building a robust professional network can significantly bolster your career trajectory. For those simultaneously navigating work and college, the academic environment offers a plethora of networking opportunities. This chapter breaks down the nuances of effective networking, weaving in narratives to illuminate pathways for impactful connections.

Laying the Groundwork: Understanding the Power of Networking

Expanding Opportunities:

A well-knit network can open doors to jobs, collaborations, and unique professional opportunities.

Story Insight: Aisha, a finance major working in a small firm, landed a dream job at a multinational company through a connection she made during a college seminar.

Diverse Perspectives:

Networking exposes you to a mosaic of perspectives, refining your outlook and enhancing your problem-solving capabilities.

Story Insight: Jake, a graphic designer branching into advertising, tapped into his college network to gather diverse campaign ideas, enriching his portfolio.

The Campus: A Networking Goldmine

Engage in College Clubs & Organizations:

Being active in extracurricular activities not only broadens your skill set but also exposes you to potential mentors and peers.

Story Insight: Mia, a computer programmer studying software engineering, connected with industry pioneers through her college coding club, gleaning invaluable insights.

Alumni Events:

Alumni often willingly support current students, offering guidance, mentorship, or job opportunities.

Story Insight: Leo, an HR executive studying organizational psychology, rekindled a connection with an alumnus at a college event, leading to a collaborative project between their respective firms.

Effective Networking: Beyond Handshakes and Business Cards

Authentic Interactions:

Genuine, interest-driven conversations often create deeper connections than superficial exchanges.

Story Insight: Fatima, a biologist diving into genetic research, formed lasting bonds at a conference, not by pushing her agenda, but by authentically discussing her passion for genetics.

Follow-up & Nurturing:

Networking isn't a one-off event. Regularly touch base with your connections, updating them on your progress and helping when possible.

Story Insight: Samuel, an entrepreneur studying sustainable solutions, maintained a ritual of sending biannual updates to his network, leading to several collaborative ventures.

Merging Work and College Networks

Cross-Pollinate Ideas:

Introduce connections from work to those from college and vice versa, fostering a fertile ground for collaboration.

Story Insight: Clara, a data analyst exploring AI, introduced her professor to her work supervisor, culminating in a groundbreaking joint project.

Leverage Academic Projects:

Use class assignments or projects as an opportunity to collaborate with or seek feedback from work connections.

Story Insight: Andrei, a journalist covering international relations, worked on a college paper about trade policies, refining it through insights from his professional contacts.

Networking, often misconstrued as a mere exchange of contacts, is an art that requires tact, authenticity, and persistence. This chapter, through tales and techniques, aims to demystify the process and offer actionable insights. As you traverse the dual worlds of work and college, a robust network can be your compass, guiding you towards uncharted opportunities and enriching experiences.

Chapter 18: Managing Stress and Avoiding Burnout

"Almost everything will work again if you unplug it for a few minutes, including you." - Anne Lamott

Balancing the demands of a full-time job with academic rigor is no walk in the park. Such a life can present multifaceted challenges, with stress and burnout looming large if not managed effectively. This chapter delves into strategies to understand, combat, and even harness stress, intertwining insights with relatable narratives to provide a comprehensive guide on maintaining mental equilibrium.

Recognizing the Signs: The Silent Creep of Burnout

Physical Symptoms:

Exhaustion, sleep disturbances, and frequent illnesses can all indicate burnout.

Story Insight: Ravi, a bank executive pursuing an MBA, ignored his recurring migraines and fatigue, attributing them to 'just another busy week.' It took a medical leave of absence to realize he was burnt out.

Emotional & Mental Symptoms:

Feelings of detachment, chronic frustration, and reduced performance often accompany burnout.

Story Insight: Gabriella, a nurse furthering her medical studies, found herself growing resentful of her patients, a stark contrast to her usual empathetic self. She recognized this as a sign of emotional exhaustion.

Proactive Stress Management: Building Resilience

Establish Boundaries:

Clearly define work, study, and personal time. This compartmentalization can be a buffer against encroaching stressors.

Story Insight: Hassan, a software developer studying user experience design, set a strict rule of no work emails after 7 pm, allowing himself the evening to study or relax.

Regular Self-Assessment:

Periodically gauge your stress levels, reflecting on what's manageable and what adjustments might be required.

Story Insight: Larissa, an educator working towards her doctoral degree, maintained a stress diary, logging triggers and her responses, aiding in proactive stress management.

Holistic Health: A Pillar Against Burnout

Physical Wellness:

Regular exercise, a balanced diet, and adequate sleep are non-negotiables.

Story Insight: Keegan, a journalist exploring broadcast media, took up morning runs. This habit not only boosted his energy but also became a meditation of sorts, clearing his mind for the day ahead.

Mental & Emotional Wellness:

Practices like meditation, journaling, and seeking therapy can be essential tools.

Story Insight: Ayesha, an engineer venturing into sustainable technologies, started bi-weekly therapy sessions, providing her a safe space to vent and gain perspective.

Leveraging Support: You're Not Alone

Peer Support:

Engage with fellow students who are juggling work and studies. They can offer camaraderie, insights, and even study partnerships.

Story Insight: Pierre, a chef exploring culinary arts academically, formed a study group with fellow working students. They shared resources, study tactics, and much-needed empathy.

Seek External Resources:

Many colleges offer counseling services, workshops, or seminars on stress management and time management.

Story Insight: Wan, an artist delving deeper into art history, attended a stress management workshop at her college, gleaning techniques that transformed her approach to her busy schedule.

Stress, an inevitable component of our fast-paced lives, need not escalate to burnout. With awareness, proactive strategies, and a commitment to holistic well-being, it's entirely possible to navigate the demanding terrains of work and college without succumbing to overwhelming pressure. This chapter, with its blend of tales and tactics, seeks to illuminate a path of balanced vigor, where stress becomes not a bane but a catalyst for growth.

Chapter 19: The Benefits and Challenges of Weekend Classes

"The key is not to prioritize what's on your schedule, but to schedule your priorities." - Stephen Covey

Weekend classes have emerged as a beacon of hope for those balancing work and academics. But just as they offer flexibility and cater to the busy schedules of working students, they come with their unique set of challenges. This chapter dives deep into the world of weekend academics, interspersing practical insights with compelling narratives, ensuring that readers get a holistic view of what it means to trade weekend relaxation for classroom learning.

The Lure of Weekend Classes

Fits the 9-to-5 Schedule:

For those bound by the typical weekday work schedule, weekend classes offer a convenient avenue to pursue higher education without conflict.

Story Insight: Nina, a marketing professional, found that weekend classes allowed her to seamlessly integrate her pursuit of an MBA without compromising her work.

Intensive Learning:

Condensed into fewer days, weekend classes often promote a focused and immersive learning environment.

Story Insight: Carlos, an architect delving into sustainable building solutions, appreciated the deep dives his weekend modules offered, letting him grasp complex concepts without daily interruptions.

The Flip Side: Potential Pitfalls

Compromised Leisure Time:

With classes occupying weekends, personal downtime, and family commitments can take a hit.

Story Insight: Lydia, a single mother and legal assistant, often found herself juggling between her law classes and spending quality time with her son on weekends.

Potential for Burnout:

With no real 'break' between work and school, the continuous cycle can lead to quicker burnout.

Story Insight: Omar, an IT consultant, began feeling overwhelmed by the relentless rhythm of transitioning from weekday work pressures to intense weekend classes.

Making the Most of Weekend Academia

Proactive Planning:

Effective time management ensures that while weekdays and weekends are packed, they are also productive.

Story Insight: Yasmine, a journalist, made sure to prep for her weekend classes during the week, allowing for more active participation and reduced Sunday-night stress.

Regular Breaks:

During long class hours, ensure you take short breaks to stretch, hydrate, and mentally relax.

Story Insight: Theo, delving into digital advertising, formed a ritual with classmates: a ten-minute walk after every 90 minutes of class, ensuring they returned refreshed.

Finding Balance: Preserving Personal Time

Prioritize Self-Care:

Even amidst the bustle, carving out time for oneself—be it a short meditation, a hobby, or just a quiet coffee break—is crucial.

Story Insight: Jia, an accountant furthering her studies, ensured she had an hour of 'me-time' on Saturday mornings before her classes—a ritual that kept her centered.

Communicate with Loved Ones:

It is essential to keep family and friends in the loop, ensuring they understand and support your academic commitments.

Story Insight: Leo, a store manager pursuing business studies, had open conversations with his partner about his weekend commitments. This understanding helped them cherish and maximize their shared moments.

Embracing weekend classes is a conscious decision to prioritize academic growth, but it need not come at the cost of personal well-being or relationships. By recognizing the advantages and potential pitfalls, and by implementing initiative-taking strategies, it's possible to strike a balance. Through its tapestry of stories and insights, this chapter aims to provide both a realistic view and a roadmap for those venturing into the domain of weekend academics.

Chapter 20: Seeking Help: Tutoring, Counseling, and Other Resources

"Ask for help. Not because you are weak. But because you want to remain strong." - Les Brown

The journey through college, especially while working full time, can sometimes feel like navigating a maze. The path is riddled with academic challenges, emotional hurdles, and time-management puzzles. But remember, you do not have to traverse this maze alone. Universities and communities offer numerous resources, from academic assistance to mental health support. This chapter unveils these resources, weaving in personal narratives to showcase how seeking help can transform the collegiate experience.

Academic Aids: Beyond Classroom Learning

Tutoring Services:

These can offer clarity on complex subjects and provide personalized attention.

Story Insight: Raj, an engineer diving into advanced physics, found himself struggling with quantum mechanics. Weekly sessions with a tutor not only clarified his doubts but also deepened his passion for the subject.

Study Groups:

Collaborative learning can foster deeper understanding and diverse perspectives.

Story Insight: Aisha, an accountant, formed a study group for her finance course. Their weekly discussions enriched her grasp on concepts and gave her varied problem-solving approaches.

Emotional and Psychological Support: Navigating the Mental Maze

Counseling Services:

Colleges often provide counseling to help students manage stress, anxiety, and other emotional challenges.

Story Insight: Damien, a full-time salesman pursuing literature, grappled with imposter syndrome. Through counseling, he learned to value his unique perspective and found confidence in his academic abilities.

Support Groups:

Interacting with peers facing similar challenges can be therapeutic and provide a sense of belonging.

Story Insight: Clara, juggling her managerial role with an MBA, joined a support group for working students. Sharing struggles and triumphs with her peers became a cathartic experience, reminding her she wasn't alone.

Additional Campus Resources: Broadening Your Support Net

Career Centers:

These hubs can guide students in aligning their studies with professional aspirations, offering resume reviews, mock interviews, and networking events.

Story Insight: Andrei, an IT specialist venturing into management, sought his career center's help. Their guidance helped him land an internship, turning classroom theories into practical skills.

Workshops:

From time management to academic writing, workshops can provide targeted skills to enhance the college journey.

Story Insight: Marisol, a nurse advancing her medical knowledge, attended a research methodology workshop. It armed her with skills to approach her thesis systematically.

The Power of Asking

Engaging Professors:

Establishing a rapport with faculty can lead to valuable mentorship, clarifications on course material, and even research opportunities.

Story Insight: Tariq, a journalist exploring political science, consistently interacted with his professors during office hours. This not only clarified his academic queries but also led to a research assistant position.

Leverage Alumni Networks:

Alumni can offer insights on course relevance, post-collegiate opportunities, and practical advice on juggling work and studies.

Story Insight: Nadia, an entrepreneur deepening her marketing insights, reached out to alumni from her program. Their real-world applications of the coursework proved invaluable to her business strategies.

Every challenge encountered in the work-college balance can be surmounted with the right tools and guidance. This chapter, through its array of stories and resources, emphasizes the importance and effectiveness of seeking help. By reaching out, not only do students ensure their academic and emotional well-being, but they also enrich their overall collegiate experience.

Chapter 21: Celebrating Small Wins: The Importance of Recognizing Achievements

"Success is the sum of small efforts, repeated day in and day out." - Robert Collier

In the hustle of juggling a full-time job and college, the journey can sometimes feel like an endless marathon, each day blurring into the next. But every mile in this marathon comprises little steps, and each step signifies progress. It is crucial to pause, acknowledge, and celebrate these steps. This chapter underscores the importance of recognizing small achievements and highlights through poignant narratives how these moments of celebration can fuel motivation and bolster self-worth.

Why Celebrate Small Wins?

Motivation Multiplier:

Recognizing and celebrating small achievements serves as positive reinforcement, encouraging continued effort and dedication.

Story Insight: When Diego, a bank clerk diving into finance, solved a particularly tough equation, he treated himself to his favorite dessert. This ritual became his motivation during challenging assignments.

Building Self-Worth:

Every achievement, no matter its size, is a testament to one's capabilities and resilience.

Story Insight: Every time Mia, a graphic designer exploring art history, finished reading a dense chapter, she would add a colorful sticker to her planner. This visual representation bolstered her confidence in her academic pursuits.

Ways to Recognize and Celebrate Achievements

Maintain a Success Journal:

Document every achievement, allowing for reflection and providing a boost during challenging times.

Story Insight: Luke, an IT specialist venturing into software development, kept a journal. On days he felt overwhelmed, revisiting his successes rekindled his passion and determination.

Share with Your Support System:

Sharing achievements with loved ones magnifies the joy and provides external validation.

Story Insight: Elise, a store manager pursuing a degree in business administration, would share her academic wins with her family. Their pride in her accomplishments fueled her onward.

Redefining Success: Beyond Big Milestones

Valuing Consistency:

Maintaining a consistent effort, even if it does not lead to immediate tangible results, is an achievement.

Story Insight: Aman, a salesperson studying marketing, may not have topped his class, but his consistent efforts ensured he never missed a deadline. He celebrated this consistency with monthly movie nights.

Overcoming Personal Barriers:

Personal growth often involves breaking self-imposed limitations, and recognizing these moments can be immensely empowering.

Story Insight: Hana, a journalist battling her fear of public speaking in her communications course, gave her first successful presentation. She marked this win by attending a workshop to hone this newfound skill.

Avoiding the Comparison Trap

Your Journey, Your Pace:

With varied responsibilities, every working student's journey is unique. It's essential to focus on personal growth rather than comparing with peers.

Story Insight: As Carla, a nurse expanding her medical knowledge, saw classmates excel, she felt disheartened. But when she reflected on her own growth—balancing shifts and studies—she realized her journey was equally commendable.

Cherishing Personal Stories:

Every small win has a story—a challenge faced, an obstacle overcome, a lesson learned.

Story Insight: Idris, a barista enthusiastic about literature, might not have penned the best essay, but every paper submitted had a tale of late-night shifts, fatigue battles, and undying passion.

The chapter serves as a gentle reminder that in the demanding dance of work and college, every step forward, no matter how minuscule, is significant. By recognizing and celebrating these steps, one not only keeps the motivation alive but also crafts a collegiate journey filled with pride, joy, and self-assuredness.

Chapter 22: The Power of Passion and Keeping Your 'Why' Clear

"Passion is energy. Feel the power that comes from focusing on what excites you." – Oprah Winfrey

Juggling a full-time job with college is an incredible feat. It's an intricate ballet of deadlines, responsibilities, aspirations, and fatigue. However, what sets the rhythm, what keeps one on their toes despite the challenges, is passion. Passion for learning, growing, and advancing. Yet, just as crucial as passion is clarity: understanding why you chose this path. This chapter delves deep into the significance of passion and the clarity of purpose in sustaining motivation and navigating challenges.

Understanding the 'Why'

Anchor in Stormy Seas:

Knowing why you embarked on this dual journey serves as an anchor, grounding you during tumultuous times and reminding you of your bigger vision.

Story Insight: Clara, a call-center executive pursuing psychology, had days when assignments piled up, and shifts stretched long. But remembering her dream to become a counselor for at-risk youth gave her the strength to push through.

Guiding Light:

Your 'why' can serve as a compass, guiding decisions and priorities.

Story Insight: Raj, a mechanic exploring aerospace engineering, had to occasionally decline overtime to focus on his studies. Remembering his dream to design aircraft kept him steadfast in his choices.

Reigniting Passion

Continuous Learning:

Branch out and learn beyond the syllabus to keep the passion for your field alive.

Story Insight: Sarah, an executive assistant diving into corporate law, would attend seminars and webinars unrelated to her coursework but connected to her passion.

Connecting with Like-Minded Individuals:

Engage with peers, professionals, and enthusiasts in your chosen field to fan the flames of your passion.

Story Insight: Hamza, a retail manager studying business analytics, joined forums and discussions on emerging trends, keeping his passion ignited.

When Passion Meets Roadblocks

Re-Evaluation:

If the journey becomes too overwhelming, it might be time to revisit and adjust your 'why', ensuring it's aligned with your current aspirations and life stage.

Story Insight: Tasha, a dancer venturing into physical therapy, realized her initial 'why' was to help injured dancers. But over time, her vision evolved to establishing community rehab centers.

Seeking Inspiration:

When enthusiasm wanes, look for external sources of inspiration like books, documentaries, or mentor talks.

Story Insight: Kei, a chef branching into nutrition science, watched documentaries on global food habits, rekindling his drive.

Embracing Evolving Passions

Being Adaptable:

Passions can evolve, and it's vital to adapt and reshape your 'why' accordingly.

Story Insight: Marco, a librarian delving into literature, started with a love for classics but gradually grew passionate about contemporary works, reshaping his academic focus.

Honoring Past Commitments:

Even if passions shift, it's crucial to honor prior commitments, using them as learning experiences.

Story Insight: Lila, a coder exploring software ethics, found a new passion in cyber law. While she pivoted her studies, she used her coding knowledge to enhance her new pursuit.

This chapter underlines the essence of passion and purpose in the challenging dance of college and full-time work. When the beats of fatigue and overwhelm play loud, the rhythm of passion and the clarity of the 'why' keep the dance graceful, purposeful, and on course. It's this fusion of passion with purpose that transforms challenges into steppingstones, and dreams into realities.

Chapter 23: Leveraging Technology and Apps for Time Management and Study

"The number one benefit of information technology is that it empowers people to do what they want to do." – Steve Ballmer

In an age of technological marvels, tools to assist with time management and studying abound. These tools, when used effectively, can be the lifeline for students balancing a hectic work schedule with academic commitments. This chapter offers a deep dive into some of the most efficacious technologies and applications available to today's scholars, providing a roadmap for seamlessly integrating them into your life.

The Digital Calendar – Your New Best Friend

Syncing Work and Study:

Modern digital calendars, such as Google Calendar or Apple's iCal, can synchronize your work schedule, classes, assignments, and study times in one place.

Story Insight: Alejandro, a bank teller and business student, color-coded his shifts, lectures, and study hours, giving him a visual representation of his week.

Alerts and Reminders:

Setting reminders for upcoming due dates, exams, or even study breaks can alleviate the mental load of having to remember every detail.

Story Insight: Naomi, a nurse diving into advanced medical studies, set reminders for medication courses she had to take, intertwined with her regular class notifications.

Study and Productivity Apps

Flashcard Apps (e.g., Anki, Quizlet):

Digital flashcards allow students to study on the go, taking advantage of any free moment – during commutes, breaks, or waiting times.

Story Insight: Rajeev, an IT professional exploring cyber-security, used Quizlet to test himself on protocols during his train rides.

Note-Taking & Organization (e.g., Evernote, Notion):

Digital notebooks offer students a methodical way to store, categorize, and retrieve their notes. Some even come with collaboration features.

Story Insight: Li, a marketing associate branching into design, organized her design ideas and inspiration clippings using Evernote.

Task Managers (e.g., Todoist, Trello):

These apps help break down big projects into tasks and sub-tasks, making the academic journey more manageable.

Story Insight: Fatima, a teacher expanding into educational psychology, mapped out her entire thesis on Trello, adjusting timelines as she made progress.

Time Management Tools

Pomodoro Technique Apps (e.g., TomatoTimer, Focus Booster):

Using the principle of work sprints followed by short breaks, these apps can enhance productivity and focus.

Story Insight: Jamal, an engineer pursuing management studies, credited Focus Booster for helping him read dense material without feeling overwhelmed.

Time Trackers (e.g., RescueTime, Clockify):

By analyzing where time is spent, students can identify productivity sinks and optimize their schedules.

Story Insight: Elsa, a journalist working on her MA in Political Science, was startled to learn she spent over 7 hours a week on social media. A few tweaks, and she reclaimed valuable study time.

Educational Platforms and Resources

Online Libraries (e.g., JSTOR, Google Scholar):

Access to a plethora of journals, articles, and papers can enrich research and understanding.

Story Insight: Theo, a musician exploring music therapy, discovered rare journals on ancient music therapy techniques via JSTOR.

Learning Platforms (e.g., Khan Academy, Coursera):

For topics challenging to grasp, these platforms offer supplementary materials and courses.

Story Insight: Nia, a salesperson stepping into statistics, bridged her initial knowledge gaps with Khan Academy's modules.

Incorporating technology and applications into your study and time-management routine is like giving yourself a digital ally. This ally, ever-present, ensures you're always equipped, organized, and ready to tackle the academic challenges that come your way, even amidst the rigors of a full-time job. Embrace the digital age; it's here to be your support on this rewarding journey.

Chapter 24: Self-Care: It's Not Selfish, It's Necessary

"Caring for myself is not self-indulgence. It is self-preservation, and that is an act of political warfare." – Audre Lorde

In the labyrinth of lectures, assignments, work deadlines, and other responsibilities, it's easy to lose oneself. However, for true success in both the professional and academic arenas, one's well-being must be a top priority. This chapter unravels the essence of self-care, highlighting why it is not just a luxury but a necessity for those navigating the complexities of both full-time employment and college.

Understanding Self-Care

Beyond Bubble Baths:

While pampering oneself is indeed a form of self-care, the concept spans much broader. It includes any activity done deliberately to take care of our mental, emotional, and physical health.

Story Insight: Marcus, a law clerk and law student, defined his self-care as an uninterrupted hour of reading fiction every night – a break from legal texts and cases.

A Preventative Measure:

Regular self-care practices can prevent burnouts, reduce the negative impact of stress, and help you refocus.

Story Insight: Yara, a chef diving into nutrition science, found her escape in weekend nature hikes, recharging her mind and giving her a fresh start each week.

Key Components of Self-Care

Physical Care:

This encompasses sleep, diet, exercise, and even routine medical check-ups.

Story Insight: Reina, an accountant taking courses in financial analytics, integrated a 20-minute yoga routine into her mornings, boosting her energy for the day.

Mental and Emotional Care:

Activities such as meditation, journaling, or even seeking therapy play pivotal roles.

Story Insight: Luca, a theater artist studying playwrighting, discovered solace in journaling, transforming his day's anxieties into potential script ideas.

Social Connections:

Building and maintaining connections, be it with friends, family, or support groups, is vital.

Story Insight: Aisha, a pharmacist exploring genetic research, instituted a weekly video call ritual with her overseas best friend, grounding her amidst academic chaos.

Establishing a Self-Care Routine

Audit Your Current Routine:

Identify areas in your life that might be neglected or causing undue stress.

Story Insight: Mia, a project manager enrolling in an MBA, realized her prolonged screen time was causing eye strain and disrupted sleep. Her solution? An evening screen curfew and adopting blue-light glasses.

Prioritize and Schedule:

Make self-care appointments with yourself and honor them as you would any work meeting or class.

Story Insight: Diego, an architect studying urban planning, blocked out Sunday afternoons solely for gardening, an activity he loved and that brought him peace.

Stay Flexible:

It's crucial to understand that as our lives evolve, so too will our self-care needs.

Story Insight: Priya, a software developer turned computer science major, shifted from evening runs to dawn jogs when her course schedule changed, ensuring her self-care didn't wane.

Overcoming Guilt and Pushback

Debunking Myths:

Recognize that taking time for yourself doesn't mean you're neglecting your duties or commitments.

Story Insight: Carlos, a retail manager pursuing business studies, faced initial guilt over his bi-weekly massages until he realized how it drastically improved his productivity and mood.

Seek Support:

Surround yourself with understanding peers, friends, or mentors who champion the importance of self-care.

Story Insight: Jia, an elementary teacher advancing in child psychology, found support in an online community of working students, all of whom cheered each other's self-care endeavors.

When threads of work and education intertwine, it's a challenge to keep one's own fabric from fraying. Regular, intentional self-care is the thread-reinforcer. By placing yourself on your list of priorities, you not only ensure personal well-being but also enhance your capacity to thrive in both the workplace and the classroom. Remember, self-care is not a sign of weakness or indulgence; it's the bedrock of sustained success.

Chapter 25: Staying Motivated When Both Worlds Get Tough

"People often say that motivation doesn't last. Well, neither does bathing – that's why we recommend it daily." – Zig Ziglar

Juggling a full-time job and college studies is no walk in the park. There will undoubtedly be moments when the weight of both worlds feels crushing. Keeping the flame of motivation alive during these testing times is critical to persisting and eventually succeeding. This chapter dives deep into understanding motivation, exploring strategies to rekindle it when the journey becomes challenging.

The Nature of Motivation

Intrinsic vs. Extrinsic Motivation:

Understanding what drives you is fundamental. Is it an internal desire (intrinsic) or external rewards and recognitions (extrinsic)?

Story Insight: Kevin, a nurse delving deeper into medical research, was intrinsically motivated by his passion for discovering medical breakthroughs, while also being extrinsically driven by the prospect of better job opportunities.

Ebb and Flow of Motivation:

Accepting that motivation isn't constant can ease feelings of guilt or inadequacy during low moments.

Story Insight: Noelle, a marketing executive pursuing an MBA, had days filled with vigor and days of sheer exhaustion. Recognizing this pattern helped her prepare for and navigate low-motivation periods.

Strategies to Reignite Motivation

Visualize the End Goal:

Having a clear mental image of your desired outcome can serve as a powerful motivational tool.

Story Insight: Arjun, an engineer venturing into management, kept a photo of his dream university's campus on his work desk. This served as a daily reminder of his ultimate academic goal.

Break Tasks into Manageable Chunks:

Small, achievable tasks can boost confidence and give a sense of accomplishment.

Story Insight: Lila, a graphic designer exploring animation, segmented her major project into mini-tasks. Each task completion brought renewed energy to tackle the next.

Seek Inspiration:

Reading success stories, watching motivational videos, or even attending seminars can reignite passion.

Story Insight: Theo, a bank manager studying finance, found motivation in biographies of successful entrepreneurs who had overcome adversity.

Establish a Reward System:

Reward yourself for milestones achieved, no matter how small.

Story Insight: Fatima, a journalist stepping into documentary filmmaking, treated herself to her favorite dessert every time she submitted an assignment before the deadline.

Overcoming External and Internal Obstacles

Naysayers and Critics:

Limit your interaction with those who dampen your spirits and surround yourself with a positive, encouraging circle.

Story Insight: Ren, a chef aiming to write a culinary book, distanced himself from skeptical colleagues and found solace in a writers' group that cheered on his every effort.

Battling Inner Doubt:

Self-doubt is a formidable adversary. Overcome it by recalling past achievements and surrounding yourself with positive affirmations.

Story Insight: Sofia, a software developer branching into AI, kept a "victory jar" where she'd drop notes of her small daily triumphs. On tough days, reading these notes fortified her resolve.

Ensuring Sustainability

Regularly Reassess and Adjust:

Periodically check if your goals still align with your desires and values. If not, it's okay to adjust or change them.

Story Insight: Leo, a history teacher diving into archaeology, realized midway that his passion lay in teaching. He then refocused his studies on education methodologies, reigniting his motivation.

Stay Physically Active:

Physical activity releases endorphins, the body's natural mood lifters.

Story Insight: Chloe, a dancer studying physiotherapy, infused short dance breaks into her study hours, ensuring she stayed both motivated and active.

Navigating the realms of employment and academia simultaneously is like steering a ship through stormy waters. Your motivation is your compass. When the waves of doubt and exhaustion rise, it's this compass that will guide you through, ensuring you stay on course. By nurturing and rekindling your motivation, you equip yourself with an invaluable tool that will see you through to your destination. Remember, it's not about the speed but the direction, and motivation ensures you're always headed toward your goals.

Chapter 26: Internships and Job Opportunities: Blending Career and Education

"Opportunities don't happen. You create them." – Chris Grosser

For many students, college provides the dual benefit of education and real-world exposure through internships. But how does this work for someone already in full-time employment? This chapter uncovers the unique challenges and advantages of merging one's existing career with the educational opportunity's college offers, with a particular emphasis on internships and job opportunities.

The Dual Role: Employee and Intern

Why Consider an Internship?

Even with full-time employment, internships offer unique exposure to different industries, practices, or companies you might be interested in.

Story Insight: Jake, an accountant in a small firm, took an internship with a multinational corporation. This not only expanded his professional network but also gave him insights into large-scale financial operations.

Balancing Work, Studies, and Internship:

This requires impeccable time-management, commitment, and communication with all involved parties.

Story Insight: Michelle, a teacher, took a summer internship in educational policy analysis. This required her to use her vacation days, prepare lesson plans, and communicate her absence to her school.

Unlocking New Job Opportunities Through College

Networking in College:

University departments often have ties to industry professionals, giving access to job opportunities that might not be publicly advertised.

Story Insight: Raj, an engineer, discovered through his college's alumni network that a tech start-up was looking for experienced engineers for a groundbreaking project.

Transferring Skills from Current Job:

Use the skills and knowledge from your job to gain a competitive edge in new roles.

Story Insight: Lara, a content writer, leveraged her professional experience to secure a role in her college's editorial team, which later opened doors to publishing houses.

Integrating Career and Education

Job Flexibility:

If possible, discuss flexible work arrangements with your employer that allow for internships or additional studies.

Story Insight: Samuel, a bank executive, negotiated a part-time arrangement during his final college semester, allowing him to intern at a financial consultancy.

Online Internships:

The digital age offers remote internships, providing a way to gain experience without significant location-based disruptions.

Story Insight: Wei, a digital marketer, secured an online internship with an international firm, giving her global exposure without leaving her city.

The Challenges and Their Solutions

Time Constraints:

Juggling multiple commitments can be daunting. Prioritization, effective time management, and setting boundaries are crucial.

Story Insight: Aisha, a pharmacist, set specific days of the week for her internship, work, and studies, ensuring she could commit fully to each.

Potential Conflicts of Interest:

Ensure that your full-time job and internship are not in conflict, ethically or contractually.

Story Insight: Carlos, a software developer, had to get clearance from his employer before starting an internship with a tech start-up to ensure there wasn't any intellectual property conflict.

Reaping the Rewards

Broadened Horizons:

Diverse experiences can provide a more rounded professional profile.

Story Insight: Nadia, a museum curator, took an internship at an art restoration workshop. This added a unique dimension to her resume, making her a preferred candidate for larger, international museums.

Practical Application of Theoretical Knowledge:

College provides theory; work and internships provide practical application.

Story Insight: Dmitri, studying architecture while working at a construction firm, could directly apply theoretical knowledge from college on the field.

Incorporating internships and new job opportunities into a life that already balances work and study is challenging but rewarding. It offers a blend of experiences that can catapult one's career to new heights. By embracing both worlds, one can merge the foundational strength of education with the dynamic, ever-evolving landscape of the professional world, crafting a unique and robust career trajectory.

Chapter 27: Preparing for Finals and Big Projects: The Super-Busy Edition

"Success is where preparation and opportunity meet." – Bobby Unser

Final exams and major projects often bring a new level of stress for any student. For those also juggling a full-time job, the pressure can feel insurmountable. But fear not! This chapter will provide you with strategies, personal stories, and actionable tips to conquer these high-stake academic moments while balancing work commitments.

The Early Bird Approach

Starting Early:

The key is to begin preparations well before the due date. This approach reduces last-minute pressures and gives ample time for revisions.

Story Insight: Maria, a nurse by day and a psychology student by night, started preparing for her finals two months in advance. Every week, she'd dedicate an hour or two to reviewing past lectures, making the final study phase less overwhelming.

Strategic Planning

Breaking Tasks Down:

Divide your study material or project components into manageable sections.

Story Insight: Tom, working in sales while studying marketing, had a major project due at the end of the term. He broke it down into weekly tasks, ensuring he made consistent progress without any last-minute rushes.

Use Technology:

Apps like Todoist, Trello, or Notion can be invaluable in tracking tasks and progress.

Creating a Focused Environment

Dedicated Study Space:

A consistent, distraction-free environment boosts productivity.

Story Insight: Aisha, a call-center employee, created a dedicated corner in her room for study. Despite her irregular hours, the familiar setting helped her transition into study mode faster.

Time Blocking:

Allocate specific blocks of time in your daily schedule solely for preparation.

Story Insight: Raj, a full-time bank teller, blocked out 7 pm to 9 pm daily. These uninterrupted hours made a significant difference in his productivity.

Balancing Work and Study

Negotiate with Your Employer:

If possible, discuss your exam period with your employer in advance. Some might offer flexible hours or even a day off.

Story Insight: Lucy, a store manager, approached her employer about her finals, resulting in her getting morning shifts, leaving her evenings free for intense study sessions.

Avoid Procrastination at Work:

Get your work tasks done efficiently to prevent them from spilling over into your study time.

Story Insight: Ahmed, an IT specialist, ensured he tackled work projects promptly, preventing last-minute work emergencies from interfering with his study schedule.

Effective Study Techniques

Active Recall and Spaced Repetition:

These proven methods can help in retaining information more effectively.

Story Insight: Diego, studying literature while working at a publishing house, used active recall by testing himself on literary theories regularly. This ensured he remembered more during his finals.

Group Studies:

Study groups can be helpful, even for the super-busy student. They offer diverse perspectives and share the study load.

Story Insight: Mei, an accountant, formed a study group with classmates. They met once a week, ensuring she stayed on track with her preparations.

Health and Well-being

Take Regular Breaks:

The Pomodoro technique, 25 minutes of study followed by a 5-minute break, can be effective.

Story Insight: Jamal, who juggled a chef job with culinary school, used the Pomodoro technique during his recipe revision, finding it kept him fresh and reduced burnout.

Stay Hydrated and Eat Well:

Proper nutrition and hydration boost concentration levels.

Story Insight: Elina, a fitness instructor and nutrition student, ensured she had a bottle of water and snacks like almonds during her study sessions to maintain energy levels.

Preparing for finals and significant projects while managing a full-time job is no small feat. But with the right strategies, dedication, and a proactive approach, success is not just possible—it's guaranteed. Remember, it's a marathon, not a sprint. Celebrate small victories along the way and always keep your end goal in sight.

Chapter 28: Transitioning to Post-Grad Life with Work Experience

"Experience is the teacher of all things." – Julius Caesar

Graduating from college is a monumental achievement, often symbolizing the end of an academic journey and the commencement of professional pursuits. For those who've balanced full-time work with studies, the transition can offer a unique blend of challenges and opportunities. This chapter illuminates the nuances of leveraging your work experience as you navigate post-grad life.

The Dual-Edge Sword of Experience

Recognition of Practical Experience:

While academic knowledge is invaluable, the hands-on experience you've acquired is a coveted asset in many industries.

Story Insight: Sofia, who worked as a junior architect while studying, found that her real-world design experience made her stand out in job interviews post-graduation.

Employers appreciated her practical insights over fresh graduates.

Bridging the Gap:

While work has provided practical experience, ensure that you've grasped essential academic theories that peers might have honed during college.

Story Insight: While Rajan excelled in his IT job, he sometimes lacked the theoretical foundation his classmates had. Post-graduation, he took a few online courses to bridge this knowledge gap.

Networking: College and Beyond

Leveraging Workplace Connections:

Your job has likely given you a web of professional contacts.

Story Insight: Carlos, a marketing student who also worked in an ad agency, leveraged his work contacts to land interviews with top-tier marketing firms after graduation.

Maintaining College Networks:

Even with work connections, don't underestimate the value of university ties.

Story Insight: Leila, a business major working in a bank, found her next job opportunity through a college friend who admired her ability to manage work and studies.

Selling Your Unique Experience

Resume Building:

Your CV should effectively combine your academic achievements with your work milestones.

Story Insight: Naomi, an engineer who worked part-time in a tech firm, merged her project experiences from both school and work in her resume, showcasing a breadth of capabilities.

Interview Strategies:

Frame your college-work balance as a strength, highlighting skills like time management, discipline, and real-world application.

Story Insight: In interviews, Omar often narrated instances where he directly applied classroom theories to his job, impressing interviewers with his practical approach.

Planning Further Education

Building on Work Experience:

If you're considering post-graduate studies, your job can guide your specialization.

Story Insight: Elise, a psychology major working in HR, chose to pursue her master's in organizational psychology, combining her passion and practical knowledge.

Financial Planning:

Your work history might provide a financial cushion or even sponsorships for further studies.

Story Insight: Alex, an accountant, was sponsored by his firm to take advanced financial courses, boosting his career trajectory.

Work-Life Integration: The Next Level

Climbing the Career Ladder:

Your dual experience can fast-track promotions.

Story Insight: While many of his peers started in entry-level positions, Aarav, with his sales job experience, was offered a mid-level post after graduation.

Seeking Balance:

The grind of college and work might be over, but the lessons from that period should guide your work-life balance moving forward.

Story Insight: Juggling nursing school and hospital shifts taught Isabella the importance of self-care, a principle she adhered to even as a full-time nurse, ensuring regular breaks and vacations.

Post-graduation is an exciting phase, offering a world of opportunities. For those with the rich tapestry of work and academic experiences, it's a chance to merge the best of both worlds. Remember, every challenge faced during your college-job juggling act has armed you with resilience, wisdom, and versatility that will remain lifelong assets. Embrace the journey ahead with confidence!

Chapter 29: Reflecting on the Journey: Growth Through Struggle

"Life does not get better by chance, it gets better by change." – Jim Rohn

The grueling journey of balancing work and college tests the mettle of the most resilient individuals. As you stand at the precipice of a new chapter, taking a moment to reflect on the myriad challenges and victories, both big and small, can offer profound insights and a sense of immense gratification. This chapter encourages introspection, focusing on the growth that emerges from life's trials.

Recognizing Your Evolution

The Strength Within:

Through balancing act, you've built a resilience that many spend a lifetime cultivating.

Story Insight: Emma recalls breaking down multiple times during her first year, trying to manage her job at a retail store with her sociology major. But by her final year, she navigated hiccups with a calm she didn't know she possessed.

Versatility in Action:

Juggling diverse responsibilities has equipped you to handle varied challenges in both academic and professional spheres.

Story Insight: Jake, an IT student who worked at a cafe, unexpectedly found that his customer handling skills immensely benefited team projects and presentations.

Appreciating the Lessons from Failures

Mistakes as Steppingstones:

Failures, missed deadlines, or lower grades were not mere setbacks but valuable lessons.

Story Insight: Aria once missed a crucial work deadline and an exam on the same day. This "failure" became the catalyst for her impeccable time management skills.

Finding the Silver Lining:

Each challenge, when reflected upon, can reveal a hidden lesson or skill acquired.

Story Insight: Missing out on social events taught Leon the importance of quality over quantity in friendships, leading him to cultivate a close-knit circle of genuine friends.

Valuable Life Skills Acquired

The Power of Prioritization:

The constant tussle between work and studies has honed your ability to distinguish between the urgent and the important.

Story Insight: Maya, juggling her marketing coursework and a demanding job, mastered the art of discerning crucial tasks, a skill that later impressed her bosses.

Balancing Multiple Hats:

Swapping roles between student and employee has granted you the ability to adapt to varied situations effortlessly.

Story Insight: Sam, an art student and bartender, became adept at shifting his mindset seamlessly, making him a favorite both among professors and customers.

Embracing the Emotional Rollercoaster

The Highs and Lows:

Beyond the practical challenges, it's crucial to acknowledge the emotional and mental toll, and more importantly, your ability to bounce back.

Story Insight: Clara remembers feeling elated upon securing an A in a tough course, only to feel crushed hours later when a work project was criticized. Yet, these oscillations strengthened her emotional resilience.

Finding Joy in Small Wins:

When life was a whirlwind, even small achievements became beacons of hope and joy.

Story Insight: For Adrian, a coffee shared with a classmate, a brief commendation from his boss, or even an evening off, became moments of pure happiness.

Reflection is not merely about reminiscing but about understanding and internalizing the growth and change that have occurred. As you stand on the cusp of the future, take this journey's lessons with you. Let them be your guiding light, reminding you of your strength, versatility, and the incredible ability to rise above even the most daunting challenges. Remember, it's not just about the destination but the transformative journey. Embrace it, celebrate it!

Chapter 30: Conclusion: The Unparalleled Strength of a Working Student

"It's not the load that breaks you down; it's the way you carry it." – Lena Horne

As we reach the conclusion of this comprehensive guide, it's paramount to recognize the Herculean strength and determination displayed by working students. You are a unique blend of determination, tenacity, flexibility, and resilience. As the curtain falls on this chapter of your life, you aren't just a graduate; you are a testament to perseverance. Let's take a moment to understand and celebrate this unparalleled strength.

Embodied Resilience

A Seasoned Warrior:

Each late-night study session after a grueling work shift, every sacrificed weekend, and every silent tear of exhaustion or frustration has forged you into an individual of immeasurable strength.

Story Insight: Daniel worked nightly shifts at a warehouse, often coming home at dawn. Even with drooping eyes, he'd hit the books. Today, as a successful engineer, he considers those early morning hours his most defining.

Duality of Roles

The Best of Both Worlds:

Wearing the dual hats of employee and student, you've experienced diverse worlds, each sharpening different facets of your personality.

Story Insight: Lila, a business student and a bookstore employee, adeptly employed her academic learnings to enhance in-store sales, while her job taught her practical business nuances.

Maturity Beyond Years

A Lifetime of Lessons:

The challenges you've navigated have imparted life lessons that many acquire much later in life.

Story Insight: At 22, Mia had negotiated with professors, managed financial crises, and tackled workplace challenges, giving her a maturity often seen in those much older.

Unwavering Commitment

A Beacon of Dedication:

Juggling academics with a job is an unfaltering commitment to your goals and dreams.

Story Insight: When Neil's peers pondered weekend plans, he was charting out work schedules and study times. This commitment reflected when Neil launched his startup soon after graduation, with a dedication that investors admired.

The Value of Sacrifice

Understanding the Price:

You've tasted sacrifice, understanding the weight of dreams and the price they demand.

Story Insight: Zoe missed countless family gatherings and friend outings. Yet, when she stood as the valedictorian of her class, the weight of her sacrifices transformed into a crown of achievement.

The Path Forward

Beyond the Horizon:

The skills, experiences, and resilience you've cultivated have set you on a trajectory for unparalleled success in both professional and personal spheres.

Story Insight: Jack, having managed a retail job and a demanding major, stepped into the corporate world with a confidence and adaptability that saw him climb the ranks with unprecedented speed.

As you flip the final page of this chapter, remember the beauty of the journey you've embarked upon. The late nights, the challenging balance, the sacrifices—all these have carved a path illuminated by lessons, growth, and a strength that stands unparalleled. As a working student, you are a beacon of hope, tenacity, and incredible capability. The world awaits your prowess, and this journey has armed you with the very best. Embrace the future, for with your unparalleled strength, the sky is merely the beginning. Celebrate yourself, for you truly are exceptional.